Cybersecurity in Finance
Getting the policy mix right

Cybersecurity in Finance

Getting the policy mix right

Sylvain Bouyon
Simon Krause

Report of a CEPS-ECRI Task Force
Chaired by
Richard Parlour

Centre for European Policy Studies
European Credit Research Institute
Brussels

Published by Rowman & Littlefield International, Ltd.
6 Tinworth Street, London, SE11 5AL
www.rowmaninternational.com

Rowman & Littlefield International Ltd. is an affiliate of Rowman & Littlefield
4501 Forbes Boulevard, Suite 200, Lanham, Maryland 20706, USA
With additional offices in Boulder, New York, Toronto (Canada) and Plymouth (UK)
www.rowman.com

Centre for European Policy Studies
Place du Congrès 1, B-1000 Brussels
Tel: (32.2) 229.39.11
E-mail: info@ceps.eu
Website: http://www.ceps.eu

Cover illustration: Shutterstock/vs148

British Library Cataloguing in Publication Data
A catalogue record for this book is available from the British Library

ISBN: 978-1-78661-217-5 Hardback
        978-1-78661-218-2 Paperback
        978-1-78661-219-9 Ebook

The European Credit Research Institute (ECRI) is an independent think tank that carries out research and contributes to the policy debate on financial services in Europe. It is managed by the Centre for European Policy Studies (CEPS), a leading think tank covering a broad range of policies in EU affairs.

This report is based on discussions in the CEPS-ECRI Task Force on "Cybersecurity in Finance: Getting the policy mix right". The group met four times between September 2017 and May 2018 under the chairmanship of Richard Parlour, Principal at Financial Markets Law International. It was established by rapporteurs Sylvain Bouyon, Research Fellow and Head of Fintech and Retail Finance at CEPS and ECRI and Simon Krause, Visiting Researcher at CEPS.

The policy recommendations offered at the beginning of this report reflect a general consensus reached by Task Force members, although not every member agrees with every aspect of each recommendation. A list of Task Force members, observers and invited guests can be found in the Annex. The members were given the opportunity to comment on the draft final report, but its contents may only be attributed to the rapporteurs and do not necessarily represent the views of the institutions to which the members belong.

CONTENTS

Boxes and Tables

ABBREVIATIONS

CSIRT	Computer Security Incident Response Team
DoS	Denial-of-service
EBA	European Banking Authority
ECB	European Central Bank
ECRB	Euro Cyber Resilience Board
ENISA	European Network and Information Security Agency
eIDAS	Electronic identification, authentication and trust services
G-SIB	Global systemically important bank
GDPR	General Data Protection Regulation
IT	Information technology
NCA	National Competent Authority
NIS	Network Information Service
PSD	Payment Services Directive
PSP	Payment service provider
SSM	Single Supervisory Mechanism

FOREWORD

With the inexorable rise of e-commerce comes the inexorable rise of the e-criminal. Cybercrime is now the world's fastest growing crime. It has leapt to number two of the top ten business risks worldwide, from not even appearing in that list five years ago. For certain countries, cyberattack is now the risk of greatest concern. Gone are the days of concern about a low level hack of a website by a script kiddie. Today's attackers are multi-faceted and increasing in sophistication, ranging from advanced persistent threats, corporate espionage, organised crime and 'hactivists' to cyberterrorists, ever more competent, and ever better funded. Cybersecurity has moved from being a technical issue to a political and boardroom issue. Financial markets are particularly important as they oil the wheels of all member state economies.

So what should the priorities of cybersecurity be? Is the rise of cybercrime so fast and extensive that we should be changing the focus more to one of cyber resilience? There are three core themes to address:

1. Governance (at all of organisational, international and national levels)
2. Risk Management (both contextually and intelligence driven)
3. Capability (cybersecurity by design and by default, using a standard framework applied to context)

There is a multitude of issues that the financial sector needs to address. Our Task Force has chosen to focus on certain key issues rather than attempt to produce an encyclopaedic tome. Any report can only represent a snapshot in time and it will be particularly important to continue to communicate as technology and the threat advances. I hope that the work that our Task Force has undertaken in producing this report will make a valuable contribution to the advancement of cybersecurity policy and protection and safeguarding of the economies of the EU member states and the financial markets on which they depend.

Richard Parlour
Chairman of the Task Force
June 2018

EXECUTIVE SUMMARY

Amid several large cyberattacks in 2017, the European Commission adopted in September 2017 its multi-sector cybersecurity package. Whereas this initiative should contribute to strengthening the cyber-resilience and response of EU financial firms, several policy issues and unanswered questions remain. In order to analyse the issues that are considered to be relevant to financial fields (retail banking, corporate banking, capital markets, financial infrastructure and insurance), CEPS-ECRI organised a Task Force between September 2017 and May 2018 with a group of experts from the financial industry, tech industry, national supervisors and European institutions, as well from one consumer association and one law firm.

Nine more policy issues need to be further addressed in order to bolster the financial industry's cyber-resilience against current and future threats. These issues are itemised below, followed by a more in-depth discussion of each issue.

Main policy recommendations

1. Convergence in the taxonomies of cyber-incidents is needed.

2. The framework for incident reporting needs to be greatly improved to fully contribute to the cyber-resilience of financial firms.

3. Authorities should assess how and to what extent the data held by the centralised hub should be shared with supervisors, firms and clients.

4. Ambitious policies are needed to develop consistent, reliable and exploitable statistics on cyber-trends.

5. Best practices for cyber-hygiene should be continuously enhanced by regulators and supervisors.

6. The European Cybersecurity Certification Scheme needs to be strengthened to contribute better to cybersecurity, cyber-risk management and capability.

7. In order to improve the processes of attribution and extradition, the reinforcement of cross-border cooperation and legal convergence remains a priority, both within the EU and more widely.

8. Best practices in remedies in case of cyberattacks need to be further encouraged.

9. Policy-makers should further assess the pros, cons and feasibility of creating an emergency fund in case of large cyberattacks.

1. A common taxonomy for cyber-incidents

A common taxonomy across regulations, jurisdictions and sectors should ease the understanding of multi-country and multi-sector cyberattacks, and eventually strengthen the quality of responses. Given the ever-changing nature of cyberspace, the reference taxonomy should be flexible enough to be revised on a regular basis. Also, for better readability by CSIRTs, this common taxonomy should include specific sections on the variants applicable to different sectors, if relevant.

Wherever possible, convergence in templates for incident reporting is needed across legislation. However, given the diversity in the purposes of legislation, full harmonisation in those templates remains challenging.

2. Need to develop an efficient legislative and institutional framework for incident reporting

The emergence of different reporting requirements (notably in GDPR, PSD2, NIS Directive, ECB/SSM, eIDAS regulation and Target 2) raises questions about what is the most adequate cyber-incident framework for boosting the cyber-resilience of financial firms. For that purpose, regulators, supervisors and financial firms need to address five issues.

First, national templates for the NIS Directive and the GDPR should be harmonised across the EU. Secondly, large firms active in different countries need to develop adequate consolidation processes of the "overall cyber-risk" at group level. Thirdly, authorities should be able to exploit the content of incident reporting to inform and advise CSIRTs in return. For that purpose, policy-makers and firms should assess together the risks and opportunities of developing a system of standard messaging services.

Fourthly, the creation of a European sectoral hub for finance in charge of centralising all incident reports, dispatching the right information to stakeholders and advising both authorities and CSIRTs could greatly reinforce the incident reporting framework. Finally, in order to create a resilient cybersecurity framework that could efficiently handle multi-sectoral cyberattacks and prevent contagion from one sector to another, the hub should also be able to cover all the other sectors of the EU economy.

3. Sharing of the data held by the centralised hub with supervisors, firms and clients

Authorities should encourage the set-up of platforms aimed at facilitating the voluntary exchange of cyber-information between financial firms. In parallel, authorities should ensure that incident reporting requirements fully contribute to the cyber-resilience of financial firms. For that purpose, when deemed pertinent, the information contained in incident reporting should be quickly shared with the most relevant stakeholders.

First, the centralised hub in charge of incident reporting should quickly provide relevant supervisors with the right information on cyberattacks. Secondly, the hub also needs to share relevant information with financial firms, provided that the right balance is found between building up an efficient collective response to cyberattacks and safeguarding firms' interests. To provide technical assistance to those firms, the hub would need a clear mandate from regulators.

Sharing some information with firms' potential clients through the development of cyber-ratings that mirror the cyber-risk to which each supplier, and therefore their potential clients, is exposed should be based on market rather than regulatory initiatives. Whatever policy options are selected, tight security of the data managed by the centralised hub should be considered one of the main priorities.

4. The need to build a benchmark for macro statistics

The absence of a benchmark for macro statistics on cyber-trends and the poor consistency across sources raise the risk that the cyber-strategies of firms and cyber-policies are not well-founded. If a centralised framework is developed for incident reporting, robust and relevant macro statistics could be developed at national and European level.

Specifically, the creation of robust statistics on the financial impact of cyberattacks is necessary to better understand the overall impact of attacks and to adjust cyber-policies and strategies as needed. However, the complexity of measuring the financial impact at firm level has made it so far impossible to have consistent methodologies across organisations. A principle-based list should operate at EU level, with the aim of enhancing best practices to measure both "tangible" and "intangible" factors. Convergence should be achieved provided that collaboration is improved between cyber-authorities, CSIRTs, chief financial officers and chief information officers of organisations, authorities in charge of setting accountancy norms, etc.

5. Promoting cyber-hygiene

Authorities should continue to enhance best practices in terms of cyber-hygiene. Principle-based lists should be updated on a regular basis. At present they should for example include conducting adequate education and awareness activities, updating programs regularly and patching systems, creating complex passwords and changing them frequently, using micro-segmentation, multifactor authentication and encryption of sensitive data, implementing the least privilege principle, developing an adequate strategy to handle shadow IT and establishing an incident response and reporting plan.

6. **The European Cybersecurity Certification Scheme needs to be strengthened to contribute to improve cybersecurity**

Given the rising importance of digital technologies and their vulnerability to cyberattacks, authorities need to address persistent information asymmetries and the fragmentation of standards in national certifications. A European Cybersecurity Certification Scheme could be a powerful tool for reinforcing harmonisation, raising awareness and ensuring mutual recognition.

Yet the current Commission's proposal might lack practical operability and add unnecessary complexity. As the scheme's success depends on the voluntary participation of the private sector, it is imperative that its value added exceeds its costs. With too many issues left unclear, the current European Cybersecurity Certification Scheme needs to be strengthened to have a clear positive impact on cybersecurity.

7. **Reinforcing cross-border cooperation and legal convergence in order to improve the processes of attribution and criminalisation**

Authorities need to develop further a cross-border framework that facilitates the exchange of information and electronic evidence for the purpose of prevention, investigation and attribution of cross-border cybercrimes. When the cyber-criminals behind cross-border attacks are identified, there is a need for convergence in relevant national legal frameworks in order to facilitate their extradition.

8. **Enhancing best practices in remedies after cyberattacks**

Best practices in remedies in case of cyberattacks need to be encouraged by EU and national supervisors through the creation of core principles. These principles should cover the use of robust methodologies to assess the degree to which firms and/or clients share the cyber-liability. They should also help firms assess when consumer financial compensation that goes beyond the actual financial loss incurred should be provided. Finally, these principles should also provide guidelines on the best type of remedies in case of data theft without immediate financial loss.

9. **Assessing the pros, cons and feasibility of creating an emergency fund in case of large cyberattacks**

Authorities should assess further the pros, cons and feasibility of developing an emergency cyber-fund aimed at alleviating the risk of financial instability in case of major cyberattacks in the financial industry. Should the EU proceed in that direction, criteria for a cyber-incident to qualify and necessary conditions for the fund to be used will have to be well defined in advance.

The benefits and costs of the different options available to create such a fund should be carefully analysed. In particular, could existing EU funding schemes for natural disasters be extended to large-scale cyberattacks? Who should bear the costs? Would it preferable to design a fund specifically for the financial sector? Or would it make more sense to create a fund that covers all operators of essential services, as defined in the NIS Directive?

1. CHARACTERISATION OF CYBER-INCIDENTS

1.1 Definitions

Cybersecurity can be defined as a particular state, which could be qualified as "optimal", or as a collection of activities that ensures the achievement of a particular state. As defined by the Dutch Cybersecurity Supervisor (2017),[1] a system is cyber-secured when it reaches a state that is free of danger or damage caused by a disruption or failure of IT or through the abuse of IT.[2] [3] Overall, the danger or damage caused by abuse, disruption or failure may comprise a limitation on the availability and reliability of the IT, violation of the confidentiality of information stored in IT environments or damage to the integrity of that information.

---

[1] The publication can be found at www.ncsc.nl/english/current-topics/Cyber+Security+Assessment+Netherlands/cybersecurity-assessment-netherlands-2017.html.

[2] In practice, most cyber experts believe that an IT system can hardly be completely cyber-secured, as there are too many threats both external and internal to ever reach this level of comfort. Cyber-risk can be reduced but not completely eliminated.

[3] The UK's National Cyber Strategy defines cyber-security as follows: in this strategy, 'cyber-security' refers to the protection of information systems (hardware, software and associated infrastructure), the data on them, and the services they provide, from unauthorised access, harm or misuse. This includes harm caused intentionally by the operator of the system, or accidentally, as a result of failing to follow security procedures. (See Section 2.11 in: https://www.ncsc.gov.uk/content/files/protected_files/document_files/National%20Cyber%20Security%20Strategy%20v20.pdf).

According to ENISA (2017),[4] cybersecurity comprises all activities necessary to protect cyberspace, its users and impacted persons from cyber-threats. Cyberspace is the time-dependent set of tangible and intangible assets which store and/or transfer electronic information. The present report will use "cybersecurity" indistinctly as a state and as a collection of activities that ensures that state.

1.2   Types of cyberattacks in financial services

Many statistics can be found on the most common types of cyberattacks in financial and insurance services. Although differences can be observed in these statistics across sources, overall there is a broad consensus that denial of services (DoS),[5] web application attacks and payment card skimming[6] represent the vast majority of security incidents. The most common motive for these attacks is, as expected, financial, whereas a small share is driven by espionage and other purposes. For the vast majority of cyberattacks, the compromised data are credentials. Personal and payment data represent a much smaller share.

A large share of these cyberattacks has limited impact and affects only one or a few individuals. But, over the last decade, a few large-scale cyberattacks have been identified in the financial sector, with marked impact in both the short and long term. As shown in Table 1, these extensive attacks have affected a broad range of financial segments: retail payments, health insurance, investment,

---

[4] The publication can be found at www.enisa.europa.eu/publications/enisa-position-papers-and-opinions/enisa-overview-of-cybersecurity-and-related-terminology.

[5] Denial-of-service attack (DoS attack) is a cyberattack where the perpetrator seeks to make a machine or network resource unavailable to its intended users by temporarily or indefinitely disrupting services of a host connected to the Internet. Denial of service is typically accomplished by flooding the targeted machine or resource with superfluous requests in an attempt to overload systems and prevent some or all illegitimate requests from being fulfilled.

[6] Credit card skimming is the act of using a skimmer to illegally collect data from the magnetic strip of a credit, debit or ATM card. This information, copied onto another bank card's magnetic stripe, is then used by an identity thief to make purchases or withdraw cash in the name of the actual account holder.

consumer credit, credit registers, etc. It seems that any segment of the financial sector can be the target of a large-scale cyberattack.

Box 1. The Tesco Bank cyberattack: A case study of an attack directly impacting consumers

The cyberattack on Tesco Bank in the UK showed the consumer dimension of such attacks and the dependency of consumers on reliable, critical digital infrastructure. On the weekend of 5-6 November 2016, Tesco Bank customers experienced fraud on their accounts as well as blocked payment cards and accounts. About 9,000 customers had money stolen from their online banking accounts, with total losses amounting to £2.5 million. Other customers were affected by the hack through a temporary suspension of Tesco's web banking system's operations. Furthermore, cards could temporarily not be used for transactions and payments at ATMs and POS terminals.

The cyberattack damaged the bank's reputation and caused inconvenience for its customers. While Tesco Bank has borne the costs of the attack and fully refunded affected customers, the cyberattack has raised questions about the security of critical digital payment systems, such as online banking and transactions with payment cards. Tesco Bank had invested £500 million in building its online technology platform in the seven years prior to the attack. This investment did not prevent hackers from exploiting a vulnerability in Tesco's online banking system at scale.

Most cyber-experts have commented that every IT system has a weakness, even the most sophisticated ones. The general implication for consumers as well as for financial institutions is that the more online products and services are provided by banks, the more vulnerable they are to cyber-threats.

Against this background, what should the most adequate practices be? Can consumers protect themselves against these kinds of attacks? While there is no such thing as absolute protection against cyberattacks, consumers and banks need to follow the principles of cyber-hygiene, which are elaborated later in this report (see section 5.1). The case study of the Tesco Bank cyberattack, however, has demonstrated that the ability of consumers to act is constrained when the IT system of a financial institution is targeted by a sophisticated attack.

Table 1. Examples of large-scale cyberattacks affecting the financial sector

Industry	Year	Name of cyberattack	Affected institutions	Short description
Many industries (including banks)	2017	Petya	Firms and organisations around the world from different sectors, though concentrated in Ukraine	A series of powerful cyberattacks using the Petya malware began on 27 June 2017 that swamped websites of Ukrainian organisations, including banks, ministries, newspapers and electricity firms. Similar infections were reported in France, Germany, Italy, Poland, Russia, United Kingdom, the United States and Australia. ESET estimated on 28 June 2017 that 80% of all infections happened in Ukraine, with Germany being second hardest hit with about 9%. The attack supposedly originated from Russia.
Many industries (including banks)	2017	WannaCry	Firms and organisations around the world from different sectors that ran the Microsoft Windows system	The WannaCry ransomware attack was a worldwide cyberattack using a ransomware cryptoworm. The attack targeted computers running the Microsoft Windows operating system by encrypting data and demanding ransom payments in the Bitcoin cryptocurrency. It propagated through EternalBlue, an exploit in older Windows systems released by The Shadow Brokers a few months prior to the attack. While Microsoft had released patches previously to close the exploit, much of WannaCry's spread was from organizations that had not applied these or were using older Windows systems. WannaCry also took advantage of installing backdoors onto infected systems. The attack supposedly originated from North Korea.

Consumer credit association	2017	Equifax Data Breach	Equifax, a major US based credit information company	Cybercriminals attacked Equifax, one of the largest credit bureaus, in July 2017 and stole the personal data of 145 million people. It was considered among the worst breaches of all time because of the amount of sensitive information exposed, including names, dates of birth, social security numbers, and driving licenses numbers. The company only revealed the hack two months later. Since the stolen data could be used for identity theft, the data breach could have an impact for years to come. The CEO, the chief information officer and the chief security officer had to resign in the wake of the attack.
Financial institutions / Consumers	2016	Tesco Bank customer cyberattack	Tesco Bank, a British retail bank belonging to the Tesco group, which is publicly best known for its supermarkets	In November 2016, the customers of the British Tesco Bank became the victims of a sophisticated cyberattack. About 9,000 customers had money stolen from their online banking accounts, with total losses amounting to £2.5 million. All other customers were affected by a temporary suspension of Tesco's web banking system's operations in order to stop the "online criminal activity." The Tesco Bank has borne the costs of the attack and fully refunded the customers, who experienced financial losses on their accounts. Interestingly, the cause of the attack did not lie, as is typical in hijacked accounts, but hackers managed to seize on a vulnerability of Tesco's online banking platform, which was exploitable at scale.
Financial institutions / Capital markets	2016	Indian banks cyberattack	Major banks in India	A cyberattack from China resulted in a breach of data on 3.2 million debit cards issued by major banks in India. Of the cards, 2.6 million were from either Visa or MasterCard. The breach is said to have originated in malware introduced in systems of Hitachi Payment Services, enabling fraudsters to steal information.

Platform economy	2016	Uber cyberattack	Uber, the biggest car sharing company worldwide	Criminals stole the data of 57 million Uber customers through a cyberattack. The company bought back the data for $100,000, revealing the critical importance of the stolen information. Apparently, the data were not used for financial fraud or identity theft.
Financial institutions / Capital markets	2014	JPMorgan Chase data breach	JPMorgan Chase (investment bank) and Fidelity Investments (investment firm)	The cyberattack on JPMorgan Chase compromised data associated with over 83 million accounts – 76 million households and 7 million small businesses. The attack, officially disclosed in September 2014, was discovered by the bank's security team in late July 2014, but not completely halted until the middle of August. Besides JPMorgan Chase, the targets of the attack were nine other major financial institutions, but the only other company believed to have had data stolen was Fidelity Investments.
Insurance	2014	Anthem data breach	Anthem, a major health insurance company in the US	During the cyberattack, hackers stole the names, birth dates, social security numbers, home addresses and other personal information of 78.8 million current and former members and employees of the US health insurance Anthem. It is believed to have been the most severe cyberattack on an insurance company ever.
Retail finance/ Merchants and consumers	2013	Target data breach	Target, a leading US department store	Hackers got access to and stole data from credit card swipe machines out of Target's systems, including encrypted PIN numbers from debit cards. In addition, the criminals stole data on names, addresses, phone numbers and email addresses. The data breach affected 40 million debit and credit cards as well as indirectly up to 110 million Target customers.

Retail payments	2012	Visa and MasterCard data breach	Visa and MasterCard, two of the world's biggest payment service providers	In 2012, Visa and MasterCard informed their card-issuing banks about a security breach suffered by a third-party payments processor. This breach may have exposed the Track 1 and Track 2 data needed to counterfeit cards. The compromise happened sometime between 21 January and 25 February 2012, affecting up to 10 million Visa and MasterCard cards.
Financial institutions / Capital markets	2011	Citgroup data breach	Citigroup, one of the leading US financial institutions	Citigroup suffered from a major data breach in 2011, when the customer information from contact details to account numbers from over 200,000 of the bank's customers were compromised. The cyberattack resulted in a $2.7 million loss for the bank.
Data insights/ marketing	2011	Epsilon data breach	Epsilon, a provider of marketing services, loyalty programmes, web development, analytics, data services, strategic consulting and creative services	One of the costliest cyberattacks in history, the 2011 data breach at Epsilon, the world's largest provider of marketing and handling services to industry giants such as JP Morgan Chase, Best Buy, other major financial services, retailers and other companies, had an estimated damage of $225 million to $4 billion dollars. The targets of the hackers were email addresses that they could use for criminal activities, making its implications more severe than estimated.

Source: Compilation of CEPS-ECRI.

2. NEED FOR CONVERGENCE IN INCIDENT REPORTING SCHEMES

2.1 Increase in legislation with incident reporting requirements

Several recent new EU regulations and directives include incident reporting requirements in the event of a cyber-breach. The requirements for an institution or data controller to report or notify specific authorities, and in some cases the public, in the event of a cyber-breach are notably covered in the following legislation:

- General Data Protection Regulation (GDPR) in Articles 33 and 34[7]
- Payment Service Directive 2 (PSD2) in Article 96 as well as the corresponding EBA Guidelines[8]
- Directive on Security of Network and Information Systems (NIS) in Articles 6, 14 and 16[9]
- Regulation on Electronic Identification and Trust Services for Electronic Transactions in the Internal Market (eIDAS) in Article 19[10]

---

[7] The Regulation text can be found at http://eur-lex.europa.eu/legal-content/EN/TXT/PDF/?uri=CELEX:32016R0679&from=EN.

[8] The Directive text can be found at https://eur-lex.europa.eu/legal-content/EN/TXT/PDF/?uri=CELEX:32015L2366&from=EN.

[9] The Directive text can be found at http://eur-lex.europa.eu/legal-content/EN/TXT/PDF/?uri=CELEX:32016L1148&from=EN.

[10] The Directive text can be found at https://ec.europa.eu/futurium/en/system/files/ged/eidas_regulation.pdf.

- Cyber-incident reporting of the European Central Bank[11]
- TARGET2[12]

As shown in Table 2, high fragmentation can be observed between rules in taxonomy for reporting, reporting time frame, the template to be used and the threshold to trigger an incident. For instance, whereas there is no undue delay in the reporting time frame for the NIS, the deadline is 72 hours for the GDPR, 24 hours for the eIDAS and 48 hours for Target2. The template is not clearly defined in GDPR and NIS, while it is provided for the eIDAS (via document for ENISA reporting but not defined in member states) and for TARGET2 (via document in Annex II).

---

[11] Some elements on ECB incident reporting can be found at www.bankingsupervision.europa.eu/press/publications/newsletter/2017/html/ssm.nl170517_3.en.html.

[12] Some TARGET 2 elements can be found at www.ecb.europa.eu/explainers/tell-me/html/target2.en.html. Contrary to the PSD2, eIDAS, GDPR and NIS, TARGET2 is a market infrastructure rather than legislation. TARGET2 provides some guidelines that request concerned firms to notify the national central banks in case of incident.

Table 2. Conditions for incident reporting by type of rule

	GDPR	NIS	eIDAS Regulation	TARGET2	ECB (cyber-incident)	PSD2
Taxonomy for reporting	High-level guideline	N/A	Yes, provided via doc for the ENISA reporting but not in MS	Yes, provided via doc in Annex II	Yes, provided in doc sent by ECB	Yes, provided via doc
Reporting time frame	Within 72 hours	Without undue delay	Within 24 hours	Within 48 hours	Within 2 hours	Within 4 hours
Template to send report	N/A	N/A	Yes, provided via doc for the ENISA reporting but not defined in MS	Yes, provided via doc in Annex II	Excel Spreadsheet	Excel Spreadsheet
Threshold to trigger an incident	Provided via scenarios / examples in doc	Yes, provided via guideline from ENISA	Yes, provided via doc for the ENISA reporting but not defined in MS	More than 30 min limit for critical participants or up to relevancy of BCE	Yes, provided via doc sent by ECB	Yes, provided via doc

| Reporting to consumers | Yes, reporting is required if data breach is likely to result in a high risk to the rights and freedoms of affected consumers | Yes, competent authority or CSIRT may request information of consumers, if public awareness is necessary or if disclosure of the incident is in the public interest | Yes, in case of security breaches or integrity losses "adequate information" on security breaches and security risk assessments should be provided to concerned parties, including consumers | N/A | N/A | Yes, if the incident has or may have an impact on the financial interests of consumers, the PSP shall, without undue delay, inform them about the incident and measures to undertake |

Source: Compilation of CEPS-ECRI; based on information from BBVA, Intesa Sanpaolo and BEUC.

There is also great diversity in the types of authorities that have to collect incident reports (see Table 3). Some of these authorities are European bodies, such as the ECB for ECB cyber-incidents. Others are national: national NIS authorities for the NIS Directive, NCA for the PSD2 (the information is then reported to the EBA which eventually reports it to the ECB), national data protection authorities for the GDPR, national certification authority for the eIDAS Regulation and national central banks for Target2. Also, some requirements and the related authority in charge concern only financial firms: PSD2 or Target2. Some others are multisectoral: eIDAS, NIS Directive and GDPR. Finally, each piece of legislation defines a different set of criteria to determine the type of financial firm that needs to comply with the reporting requirements.

In addition to incident reporting to the competent authorities, most regulations require the notification of consumers which have been affected by a cybersecurity incident. The GDPR requires the supervisory authority, unless the financial institution has already done so, to inform consumers without undue delay if the data breach has a high risk to impact their rights and freedoms negatively. Similarly, the eIDAS Regulation requests consumer notification with appropriate information in case of major security breaches or integrity losses. The NIS Directive defines either the necessity of public awareness or public interest as the threshold for incident reporting to consumers. PSD2 requires the payment service providers to inform their affected consumers without undue delay about both the cybersecurity incident and the remedial measures if the incident has or may have an impact on the financial interests of consumers.

While these regulations all cover reporting requirements to consumers, significant heterogeneity can be observed in terms of the criteria, standards, thresholds, time frames and general approaches to consumer notification. Different interpretations across legislations might further raise the degree of this fragmentation. Moreover, the reporting requirements are characterised by discretion, meaning that for instance financial institutions are obliged to assess consumers' personal and financial risks arising from a data breach. Therefore, the consumer dimension and scope of cyber-incident reporting as well as the difficulties due to legal fragmentations should not be underestimated.

Table 3. Organisations concerned incident reporting

Requirements	Authorities	Financial firms	
		Titles	Definition
NIS Directive	National NIS Authority	Operator Essential Service (OES)	Banks and financial institutions are considered as OES because they (a) provide a service which is essential for the maintenance of critical societal and/or economic activities; (b) the provision of that service depends on network and information systems; and (c) an incident would have significant disruptive effects on the provision of that service
GDPR	National Data Protection Authority	Personal Data Processor/ Controller	Banks and financial institutions operate both as Processor, which processes personal data on behalf of the controller, and Controller which determines the purposes and means of the processing of personal data
eIDAS Regulation	National certification authority	Trust Service Providers	Banks and financial institutions can operate with their trust services either as a Qualified or as a Non-qualified trust service provider
PSD2	NCA/EBA/ECB*	Payment Services Providers	Banks and financial institutions operating as Payment Service Providers (PSPs)
ECB/SSM	ECB/Joint Supervisory Team	Significant institutions	The ECB classify a bank as Significant or Not Significant based upon the criteria of size, economic importance, cross-border activities and direct public financial assistance
ECB Target 2	National Central Bank/TARGET 2	Target 2 Participants	A distinction is made between critical participants and non-critical participants depending on the market share in terms of value and/or the type of transactions processed

* Incident reporting in the context of PSD2 has to be sent to the National Competent Authority (NCA), which sends it to the EBA, which sends it to the ECB.

Source: Intesa Sanpaolo.

2.2 Need to develop a common taxonomy for incidents reporting

The development of a common taxonomy for incident reporting is needed for various reasons. First, as cyberspace is global, cyber-insecurity is often a multi-country issue. Often, similar patterns of threat can simultaneously affect organisations located in different countries. As such, cross-border exchange of information is needed to address cybersecurity issues better and manage cyber-incidents efficiently and effectively. Fragmentation in taxonomies across jurisdictions is likely to impede the efficiency of cross-border exchanges of information, as the process of understanding the incident could be slower. As such, convergence in taxonomies should contribute to help respond to multi-country cyberattacks better.

Secondly, as shown in Table 2, there is an increase in incident reporting requirements. A standard taxonomy, adopted across all regulations and directives, regardless of whether it is on a cross-border basis, should facilitate smooth and efficient interactions between authorities and CSIRTs, especially by contributing to avoiding inconsistencies in the reported information.

In principle, the creation of a distinct taxonomy for each piece of legislation should not be justifiable. Finally, as emphasised by ENISA (2018),[13] persistent fragmentation in taxonomies will slow the emergence of automation in incident reporting and responses.

Nevertheless, the development of a common taxonomy for incident reporting faces specific challenges. First, cyberspace is constantly evolving. As a result, cyberattacks are changing on a regular basis and new forms of attacks continuously appear. A non-flexible taxonomy that sets rigid standards for long periods is therefore ill-adapted.

Secondly, existing taxonomies are often designed for specific economic sectors or companies. Organisations often have different needs and expectations. As such, CSIRTs often end up developing their own incident classifications for internal use (ENISA, 2018).

---

[13] See Reference Incident Classification Taxonomy, Task Force Status and Way Forward, ENISA, January 2018 (www.enisa.europa.eu/publications/reference-incident-classification-taxonomy).

As highlighted by ENISA (2018), one possibility for strengthening convergence in incident taxonomies is to develop a centralised repository for hosting all relevant taxonomies. Questions remain about which body should be in charge of such a task. Given the global nature of many cyberattacks, it would *a priori* make sense to design a global repository. But the development of a final consensus at the global scale might be unrealistic. Therefore, as a first step, it would be preferable to focus on an EU depository developed by the EU agency in charge of cybersecurity, namely ENISA.

The next objective would be to develop only one taxonomy that encompasses all the processes in the scope. This taxonomy should include specific sections to cover the variants applicable to the different sectors, if relevant. Given the constant changes in the type and nature of cyberattacks, the common taxonomy should also be sufficiently flexible to be continuously updated.[14]

2.3   Need to develop an efficient legislative and institutional framework for incident reporting

The emergence of different reporting requirements raises questions about the most adequate legislative and institutional framework for shaping the relationships between CSIRTs and authorities. Eventually, the objective is to ensure that the framework helps financial firms protect themselves from cyberattacks and, in case of cyberattacks, helps these firms activate timely and efficient responses.

Responses that are timely and efficient should contribute to limiting the short-term and mid-term damages to firms and, in some circumstances, are likely to prevent the expansion of attacks to other firms and sectors. The framework as developed should aim at reinforcing cyber-resilience and business continuity as much as possible. In order to do so, regulators, supervisors and financial firms should focus on the following five issues.

---

[14] For example ENISA (2018) promotes the use of "Other" or "Unknown" in the "Tag" field by the owners of taxonomies as an indicator to revise taxonomies. This field can be used if there is an increase in that category with incidents or events of the same type.

Issue 1. Convergence in templates across the EU

For each piece of legislation whose purpose is to develop incident reporting, convergence in templates should be ensured across the EU. This priority concerns mainly the NIS Directive and the GDPR, as related templates should be primarily defined at national level. As regards the GDPR, one of the roles of the Data Protection Article 29 Working Party and the future European Data Protection Board (the latter will replace the former once the GDPR takes effect, see Recital 139 of GDPR) should be to reinforce the harmonisation in those national templates.

Issue 2. Adequate governance at group level

For financial firms that have activities across different jurisdictions, high fragmentation in templates and typologies could impede the ability of CISRTs to understand the overall picture of the incidents impacting the banking group. Against this background, the banking group could be compliant with the respective incident reporting requirements at national level, while not being able to understand holistically what is at stake. Effective governance at HQ level, with adequate consolidation processes of the "overall cyber-risk" at group level, is therefore also needed. This is a key condition for the authority in charge to have a clear idea of the overall level of risks triggered by specific cyber-incidents.

Issue 3. Assessing the possibilities to develop an infrastructure with bidirectional flows

At present, all incident reporting processes are defined with a single direction flow, from CSIRTs to authorities in charge. None of the legislation emphasises or designs two-way flows. There was a broad consensus within the Task Force that a bidirectional process with respect to incident reporting will eventually be needed. In other words, authorities should be able to exploit the content of incident reporting to inform and advise CSIRTs in return.

One of the options to achieve two-way flows concerns the development of specific network infrastructure channels that provide secure messaging services. This would imply that financial firms use a common application to report incidents. The development of SWIFT messages on the interbank market could be inspirational in this respect. In the end, information about cyber-incidents could be sent and received in a secure, standardised and reliable environment.

This model should contribute to streamlining incident reporting processes. High standardisation of templates should in principle increase processing speed and response. Given that speed is one of the main criteria for coping with large-scale cyberattacks, this benefit could be precious.

However, one of the main issues to address in order to create a common application for cyber-incidents concerns the nature and type of information encoded in the message. The diversity of templates across pieces of legislation (and likely, for two of them, across countries) can be justified by the fact that each piece of legislation has a specific purpose.[15] The development of standard messages should ensure that this diversity can be replicated in that new system. The different authorities need to be able to retrieve the right information within the expected time. There is a significant risk that incident reporting based on standard messaging services might end up being too generic to be adequately exploited by CSIRTs and authorities.[16]

---

[15] Harmonisation of templates is a clear policy objective, but given the different purposes of the pieces of legislation as well as different interests pursued by national regulators, complete harmonisation will be very challenging. Yet it is worth striving for a more convergent implementation of European or international standards of templates. There are indeed possibilities for harmonisation within the existing legal framework for cyber-incident reporting. For example, parts of the Target2 template are similar to the NIS template provided by ENISA. The sections "description of the incident", "cause of the incident" and "remedial action" in the Target2 template are likely the same information as the sections "general description of the security incident", "detailed causes" and "mitigating security measures" of the corresponding NIS template. Therefore, European harmonisation should start within the existing regulations and their templates, taxonomies and reporting standards before the policy process can move on to cushion the fragmentation between the different templates.

[16] An example of such incident reporting based on standard messaging services is SWIFT's Customer Security Programme (CSP), which legally requires all participating financial institutions to report and share their information on cyber-threats and incidents as soon as they have occurred. In the case of SWIFT, the CSP is supported by an "Information Sharing and Analysis Centre" to exploit the gathered data for data sharing and analysis. It was not possible to

Should the financial sector decide in any event to go in that direction, questions would remain about the funding of such an application: Should it be funded by financial firms? by governments, for the sake of cybersecurity? Or should it be a hybrid model combining both funding channels?

Issue 4. Assessing the possibility of developing a centralised hub

A hub should be developed with the objective of centralising all incident reports and dispatching them to the right authorities. The hub could be in charge of incident reporting for the whole financial sector and handle relationships with all concerned authorities, regardless of whether these authorities are national or European, and cover all sectors or only the financial sector. In return, the hub would be in charge of informing and advising financial firms on cyber-incidents. By centralising all incident reports for the financial sector, the hub would have a broad and clear picture at any given time of the cyber-risks in this sector. Strong analytical capabilities would be needed in this respect. The purpose would not be to have a hub that is only a dispatcher of incident reports.

The hub could also play the role of coordinator between, on the one hand, all authorities in charge and, on the other hand, authorities and CSIRTs. Given the global nature of cyber-insecurity, the hub should be established at European level. The mandate of existing European agencies such as ENISA could be significantly extended to cover these complex tasks or a new agency could be built from scratch to focus primarily on these attributes.

A priori, the former option that builds upon the existing institutional framework would be preferable. The objective is to avoid the multiplication of EU agencies that cover broadly similar topics. But, in order to be able to handle all reporting requirements and distribute key information to the right stakeholder, the chosen agency will need a large amount of resources in terms of staff and budget. In order to fulfil its mission of technical adviser, the centralised hub would also need a clear mandate from regulators.

---

identify the extent to which this mechanism is used, but based on preliminary evidence current usage is likely limited.

Issue 5. Assessing the possibility of covering all economic sectors

So far, many of the recorded large-scale cyberattacks not only have affected more than one country; they have also disrupted more than one sector. The institutional framework therefore needs to handle a multi-sectoral dimension. The objective is to ensure that any cyberattacks are confined to one or a few firms in a specific sector and do not spread to others. If there is for example a high risk of a cyber-incident spreading from the energy sector to the financial sector, the supervisor should be able to provide real-time information to financial firms on the nature of the attack and, if possible, on the best way to respond to it.

Two options can be considered to cover the multi-sectoral dimension of cyberattacks. The first is to build a centralised hub that is in charge of all sectors including the financial one. The second concerns the establishment of a multi-sectoral network for cyber-incidents where one hub is developed for each sector of the economy: finance, energy, telecommunications, food, etc. Each hub would be in charge of one given economic sector for everything that relates to the dispatching of incident reports, notification and advice of firms in return, coordination of all stakeholders, etc.[17] In order to handle multi-sectoral attacks, a network of sectoral hubs would be established, preferably at European level, with a hub of hubs.

The preferred option should be the centralised hub for the whole EU economy. One of the main risks of a network of sectoral hubs is the development of sectoral silos that struggle to find agreement on relevant topics. The quality of information sharing processes might also decrease in a network of hubs, given the greater complexity of such processes and the greater risks of some sectoral hubs being unaware of the need to provide the right information to the right counterpart. The establishment of a centralised hub for the whole economy would nonetheless require expertise from the different sectors in order to properly understand the peculiarities.

---

[17] For the financial sector, given the existing distribution of tasks between multiple supervisors (national central banks, European central bank, twin-peak models including one supervisor for the macro-prudential part and another for micro-prudential tasks, etc.), the development of a new body to cover the tasks of a sectoral hub at the European level might be the preferred option.

3. OPTIMISING INFORMATION SHARING

3.1 Different models of information sharing

As analysed in chapter 2, an important pillar of the proposed new European hub for cyber-incidents should be incident information sharing across different stakeholders. Financial firms and supervisors would benefit from sharing such information, in the form of higher reactivity on the regulatory side and stronger cyber-resilience capabilities on the financial sector side. Questions remain about how and to what extent customers could benefit from this information sharing.

Currently, there are three leading models of cyber-incident information sharing in place across Europe. Firstly, industry-led incident information sharing schemes are based on the voluntary participation of financial institutions. For example, the members of the "Investment Banking Special Interest Group for Information Security" voluntarily share their knowledge of emerging risks and threats with other firms of the financial sector.[18] Additionally, on a global and cross-sectional basis, there is the "Financial Services Information Sharing and Analysis Centre", which functions as a leading industry group for reducing cybersecurity threats facing the financial sector.[19] Regulators or supervisors are not part of this incident information sharing scheme.

---

[18] See, for example www.ingwb.com/themes/cybersecurity-articles/tackling-cybercrime_a-shared-threat-needs-a-shared-response.

[19] See www.fsisac.com/about.

Secondly, European as well as national regulators and supervisors gather data on cybersecurity incidents based on current regulatory requirements. In particular, this concerns the NIS Directive, GDPR, eIDAS, PSD2, and the ECB with the SSM and Target 2. Within regulators and supervisors, incident data can be stored and combined, yet the information is generally not shared with the wider financial sector.

Thirdly, two-way cyber-incident information sharing can be facilitated by models of cooperation between authorities and the financial sector. Under such a scheme, information sharing and analysis centres (ISACs) collect information on cyber-threats and enable data sharing between the private and the public sector.[20] An example for such a joint initiative is the "Cyber Security Information Sharing Partnership" in the UK, which effectively links financial firms to their peers and technical advice from the National Cyber Security Centre in the UK.[21] Another example concerns the ECB which recently established the Euro Cyber Resilience Board (ECRB) for pan-European Financial Infrastructures.[22] According to a recent study conducted by the World Bank, joint initiatives of the public and private sectors are the best practice in cybersecurity reporting and incident information sharing. Regulators are expected to establish common risk and incident taxonomies as well as requirements for cybersecurity reporting, based on which information sharing can be facilitated.[23]

Therefore, the model for incident information sharing developed in this chapter is a centralised hub for incident reporting,

---

[20] See www.enisa.europa.eu/publications/information-sharing-and-analysis-center-isacs-cooperative-models.

[21] See www.ncsc.gov.uk/cisp.

[22] The ECRB aims to enhance the cyber-resilience of financial market infrastructures and critical service providers, as well as that of the wider EU financial sector, in line with international standards. According to Mr Coeuré, this will be achieved by fostering trust and collaboration and facilitating joint initiatives whether among market players or between market players and authorities. This information can be found at www.ecb.europa.eu/press/key/date/2018/html/ecb.sp180309_1.en.html.

[23] The information can be found at www.worldbank.org/en/topic/financialsector/brief/cybersecurity-cyber-risk-and-financial-sector-regulation-and-supervision.

which should be set up by supervisors and combine the different pieces of legislation (as highlighted in chapter 2). On the basis of this centralised hub, two-way cyber-incident information sharing between regulatory authorities and the financial sector can be established. This approach should raise markedly the positive contribution of legal reporting requirements to the cyber-resilience of financial firms and ensure that such requirements do not only constitute an umpteenth compliance rule.

A large amount of valuable information that is not required in the forms of an incident reporting exercise is exchanged within the first model of voluntary participation of financial firms. The set-up and development of such platforms need to be constantly encouraged by supervisors, as they are a precious complement to the model based on incident reporting requirements. In theory, the development of two parallel and non-interactive models for cybersecurity information sharing is suboptimal, as it might raise the complexity and fragmentation of information sharing. But, given the rapid change in cyber-trends, the existence of two parallel models might be needed to ensure sufficient flexibility and reactivity to changes in cybersecurity and related challenges.

3.2 Sharing of relevant information with different types of stakeholders

3.2.1 With other regulators and supervisors

Provided that it has sufficient analytical skills at its disposal, a centralised hub managing reported cyber-breaches for the whole financial sector should be able to better understand cyber-risks on a continuous basis. Fast response in the sharing of information on risks with other relevant supervisors will be key to developing a robust cyber-risk response framework. By receiving relevant information, policy-makers could also have a better view on emerging threats, thereby calibrating their policies in a more adequate manner.

3.2.2 With other financial firms

As emphasised in "Priority 3" of section 2.3, the objective of the new infrastructure for incident reporting should be to develop bidirectional flows. This notably implies that the hub in charge of gathering information on cyber-incidents could share relevant information with other firms. The frontier between what is deemed "relevant" and what is not will be at the discretion of the centralised hub.

As the relevant information most likely comes from one or a few of the financial firms, this body should carefully choose the information to share between companies, by ensuring that the right balance is found between building up an efficient collective response to cyberattacks and safeguarding firms' interests. To put it in another way, the sharing of this information should for example help other firms protect themselves from an ongoing cyberattack, whilst at the same time not distorting competition between those firms and not providing firms with information on their competitors that could be used unfairly.

The sharing of information with firms for the purpose of better protection against cyberattacks could be perceived as technical advice. The hub in charge of providing this type of information will therefore need a clear mandate from regulators to fulfil the mission of a technical adviser.

3.2.3 With potential clients of financial firms

The opportunities offered by a centralised hub should also be assessed with respect to bank clients. Typically, there has been an information asymmetry between clients and their financial providers regarding the degree to which the latter's IT systems are cyber-secured. In other words, clients have had relatively poor information on the cyber-risks to which their financial suppliers are exposed.

By forcing firms to inform consumers of breaches of their data, the GDPR should increase transparency between consumers and their suppliers for cybersecurity matters. However, when consumers are looking for a provider, they have little information on how often and to what extent each supplier has been the victim of cyberattacks, excluding media reports.

One possibility would be to assess if the data managed by the hub can be used to build specific ratings mirroring the cyber-risk to which each supplier, and therefore its clients, is exposed. Should the sample of cyber-incidents recorded by the hub be sufficient, labels could be elaborated in order to reinforce the protection of consumers and corporations which use financial services. A potential rating may focus on two different aspects of the cyber-issue:

- "process" focus: the labelling process could assess the quality of the processes used by the financial firms to alleviate cyber-risks related for example to data breaches;

- "result focus": while the "process focus" option places the emphasis on the quality of the means used by the financial firms to limit cyber-risks, the "result focus" essentially considers results. The latter can for instance reflect the number and gravity of cyberattacks that have affected the firm in the previous year.

External ratings on the cyber-risks to which financial firms are exposed could generate different advantages, especially by addressing some market dysfunctions. For clients, such a practice should contribute to alleviating the risk of moral hazard sparked by information asymmetries with respect to cybersecurity. Furthermore, the choice made by clients should be eased with a consistent methodology of assessment across the financial sector. As regards financial providers, external ratings could help the best performing ones to highlight the benefits of their offers when compared to those of their competitors. It could eventually encourage more firms to raise their cybersecurity standards.

Nevertheless, the implementation of external ratings systems can trigger significant risks and disadvantages. First of all, the effectiveness of external ratings as a communication tool can be questioned. For example, in the food industry, the use of labels for clients has often been revealed as inconsistent. In addition, some clients may simply lack interest in the information provided by the label. Even though clients may be interested in the rating, many clients might find the use of ratings difficult, as they contain too much information, much of it being not understood, confusing and poorly presented.

If customers do not trust the body providing ratings on the cybersecurity of financial firms, such external ratings might even be counterproductive. The reputation and credibility of the external assessor are therefore essential to ensuring a proper rating system.

Finally, and this might be the main argument, there is a great risk that the use of cyber-ratings could destabilise even further those financial firms with lower ratings. Low ratings could provide incentives for cyber-criminals to launch other attacks on firms with IT infrastructure that has been assessed as weak. Financial firms that have been affected by a significant cyberattack could also see their rating decrease rapidly as more attacks follow. In this context, there is a great risk that the value of such ratings could prove to be too volatile to be exploitable.

Overall, given the number of risks and drawbacks, it is likely too early for supervisors and regulators to develop such tools. The creation and use of cyber-ratings should be based on market initiatives, not regulatory ones. Should cyber-ratings be offered, supervisors should nonetheless ensure monitoring of their negative effects.

3.3   Need for a high level of protection of data held by the EU hub

The data held by the centralised hub itself would require a high level of security. With reference to the reporting standards prescribed by the EBA guidelines in Annex 2,[24] whether at the initial, intermediate or final report stage, the level of detail required for incident reporting would have to be carefully considered to ensure a sufficient level with which to draw meaningful conclusions and also safeguard European companies' interests. Despite this principle, however, the centralised hub would require a lot of critical information in order to be operational.

If this information were to be obtained by third parties with a malicious intent, the data held by the centralised hub would provide any wrongdoer with a concise list of all previous cyber-breaches, as well as the particular weaknesses of individual businesses or industries on an unprecedented scale. The related cyber-risk should be therefore carefully handled. To this end, the

---

[24] Annex 2 – EBA template for reporting data breaches and other security incidents (EBA/GL/2017/10).

physical security of the data handled by the hub should be considered one of the most crucial factors. Also, the hub should assess how and to which extent such data could be anonymised or aggregated, so misappropriation of data and illegitimate access to such data does not directly affect financial institutions or their customers.

Finally, questions remain as to the ability of the hub to share sensitive data with entities from outside of the EU. Large-scale cyberattacks often occur across different continents. In order to contribute to a strong global response, should the centralised hub in the EU systematically share relevant information with non-EU counterparts? To which extent, could international sharing of firms' incident data be performed? One key criterion concerns the state of data protection in the corresponding country. Some mechanisms have already been put in place by the EU for the case of personal data.[25] It will be needed to assess what type of legal mechanisms could be established for the international sharing of firms' data.

---

[25] Some of these mechanisms can be found at https://ec.europa.eu/info/law/law-topic/data-protection/data-transfers-outside-eu/model-contracts-transfer-personal-data-third-countries_en and https://ec.europa.eu/info/law/law-topic/data-protection/data-transfers-outside-eu/adequacy-protection-personal-data-non-eu-countries_en.

4. NEED FOR BENCHMARK STATISTICS ON CYBER-TRENDS

4.1 Statistics on the number of incidents

4.1.1 Other policy areas have their benchmarks

At the beginning of policy initiatives, regulators generally need accurate, consistent and verifiable statistics in order to analyse market dysfunctions and possible remedies. The consistency of statistics is necessary to conduct effective impact assessment of existing and future policies. As such, in most cases, for each main group of European policies, there is a correspondent statistical database. The ECB relies on a large set of macrodata contained notably in its Statistical Data Warehouse.[26] The analysis and reports produced by the European Commission's Directorate General for Economic and Financial Affairs use the AMECO annual macro-economic database.[27] Eurostat provides statistics for use in analysing a large sample of European and national policies: social policies (notably with the European Union Statistics on Income and Living Conditions, EU-SILC),[28] labour policies (the European labour force survey),[29] etc.

---

[26] See http://sdw.ecb.europa.eu/.

[27] See https://ec.europa.eu/info/business-economy-euro/indicators-statistics/economic-databases/macro-economic-database-ameco_en.

[28] See http://ec.europa.eu/eurostat/web/microdata/european-union-statistics-on-income-and-living-conditions.

[29] See http://ec.europa.eu/eurostat/web/microdata/european-union-labour-force-survey.

4.1.2   Cyber-criminality does not have such statistics at the moment

As regards cyber-criminality, no benchmark for statistics could be identified. Task Force members in charge of cybersecurity in their respective firms confirmed that they use statistics produced by their own organisation or by consulting firms. High fragmentation in the sources used and high diversity in the values for each specific element were observed.

What is the state of play at the moment for this issue? Article 7.7 of the Proposal for a Regulation of the European Commission on ENISA reads:

> ENISA shall prepare a regular EU Cybersecurity Technical Situation Report on incidents and threats based on open source information, its own analysis, and reports shared by, among others: Member States' CSIRTs (on a voluntary basis) or NIS Directive Single Points of Contact (in accordance with NIS Directive Article 14 (5)); European Cybercrime Centre (EC3) at Europol, CERT-EU.

Recital (26) reads:

> To understand better the challenges in the field of cybersecurity, and with a view to providing strategic long term advice to Member States and Union institutions, the Agency needs to analyse current and emerging risks. For that purpose, the Agency should, in cooperation with Member States and, as appropriate, with statistical bodies and others, collect relevant information and perform analyses of emerging technologies and provide topic-specific assessments on expected societal, legal, economic and regulatory impacts of technological innovations on network and information security, in particular cybersecurity. The Agency should furthermore support Member States and Union institutions, agencies and bodies in identifying emerging trends and preventing problems related to cybersecurity, by performing analyses of threats and incidents.

ENISA should be in charge of providing relevant analyses on trends in cybersecurity. However, no clear strategy or methodology is defined for ENISA to develop its own statistics that could be the reference for policy-makers, authorities, firms and consumers alike.

No indication is provided on the need to have consolidated statistics at European level. The risk is to continue having high fragmentation in the quoted sources and the value of their statistics. In the context of poor consistency across sources, the risk that the cyber-policies and strategies of organisations are not well-founded rises.

4.1.3 Incident reporting: Statistical parallel with offline criminality

What is the solution? Criminality is a specific case. Given its illegal nature, only part of it can be properly measured. A statistical parallel could be drawn with offline criminality. Different types of offline criminality are measured by robust macro statistics: intentional homicide, assault, robbery, kidnapping, theft, burglary, drug offences, etc.[30] The main statistical bias concerns offences that are not recorded by police. The share of unrecorded offences can vary across countries and its level is hard to assess. But, overall, macro statistics on recorded offences are extensively used by authorities to implement, justify and enforce specific policies. Granular data can often be found, notably by administrative entity: at district, city, region, country or European level.

Statistically speaking, the record of offences could be perceived somehow as a process of "incident reporting". By following a similar logic for cyber-criminality, it seems that if a centralised hub is developed for incident reporting, robust and relevant macro statistics could be developed at national and European level. The creation of robust macro statistics could be achieved only if certain conditions have been met.

4.1.4 Conditions for compiling robust macro statistics

First, as emphasised in chapter 2, a similar typology of cyber-events needs to be adopted throughout the EU and all economic sectors. This typology needs to be widely accepted by the CSIRTs community. This is the only way to develop consistent statistics across organisations, sectors and countries.

---

[30] See Eurostat crime and criminal justice statistics at http://ec.europa.eu/eurostat/web/crime/overview.

Secondly, some tools should be developed to control for statistical biases. A large share of cyber-incidents will most likely not be reported. The absence of record can be intentional, as the firms do not want to damage their reputation, or unintentional. The scale of the former should decrease with the obligation of reporting cyber-incidents within the context of the new rules analysed in chapter 2. Regular auditing that integrates the cyber-dimension is essential to ensuring that financial firms systematically comply. Unintentional absence cannot be corrected solely by statistics and will rely on the quality of internal cybersecurity systems that can continuously detect attacks.

Thirdly, questions will remain as to which body should be in charge of compiling such statistics. Should a framework based on sectoral hubs be the final institutional choice, it would make perfect sense for these hubs to be responsible for compiling and maintaining macro statistics. In that case, strong coordination would be needed to ensure methodological consistency across sectors.

4.2 Encouraging best practices for financial impact statistics

One big issue remains regarding statistics on financial impacts. This information is essential to better understanding the overall impact of cyberattacks and adjusting cyber-policies and strategies as needed. However, the complexity of the task at firm level has made it thus far impossible to have consistent methodologies across organisations.

Following a cyberattack, many factors can trigger a financial cost. They can be typically divided between "tangible" factors and "intangible" factors. Among "tangible" factors, there are revenue losses resulting from downtime, infrastructure damage, cost to implement compensation controls, technical investigation, customer breach notification, regulatory compliance, public relations, attorney fees and litigation, loss of intellectual property, etc. A typical challenge to measuring these costs concerns the time span during which they appear. Costs can indeed be triggered over many years. For instance, the identification, extradition and prosecution of criminals can take many years, resulting in recurring legal and investigation costs throughout the process.

On the other hand, "intangible" factors can also trigger significant financial impact: value of lost contract revenue, devaluation of trade name, etc. "Intangible" factors are often more difficult to measure accurately than "tangible" factors. Yet an adequate estimation of the costs resulting from intangible factors is crucial to forming an accurate picture of the overall financial impact of a successful attack.

Promoting the use of robust methodologies to quantify the overall financial impact of successful attacks should be one of the priorities of supervisors and regulators alike. A principle-based list could be developed at the EU level, with the aim of reinforcing convergence in practices at national level. This list would be particularly needed for the estimation of costs resulting from intangible factors and would encourage standardisation in damage quantification methodologies, valuation methods, etc.

Convergence should be achieved provided that collaboration is improved between cyber-authorities, CSIRTs, chief financial officers and chief information officers of organisations, authorities in charge of setting accountancy norms, etc. The possibility that information on financial impacts could be shared via incident reporting should be carefully assessed. Eventually, should convergence in financial assessment be observed, more reliable macro-data could be developed on the aggregate financial impact of cyberattacks.

5. COMPLEMENTARY POLICIES TO REINFORCE PREVENTION

5.1 Promoting cyber-hygiene

5.1.1 What is cyber-hygiene?

For financial firms it is imperative to manage and mitigate risk in the cyber-sphere. Practicing the major principles of cyber-hygiene is one of the key elements of a successful cybersecurity mix. Cyber-hygiene is defined "as a means to appropriately protect and maintain IT systems and devices and implement cybersecurity best practices". To be effective these measures of prevention, detection and action need to be attainable, accreditable and affordable.

5.1.2 Core principles

At present, the below principles could be for example emphasised. This list is not exhaustive and may change in the near future since underlying cyber-threats may change significantly in a short period of time.

Principle 1. Conduct cybersecurity education and awareness activities

The human factor is a key resource in cyber-hygiene. Therefore, the first best practice is the implementation of user education and awareness. Everyone from employees to third-party contractors needs to able to recognise cyber-threats, such as malware or phishing emails, in order to successfully prevent cyberattacks. In this regard, compliance is not enough. Instead, cyber-hygiene demands all staff to look beyond the technology and keep all of their devices safe.

Principle 2. Update programs regularly and patch systems

All systems, devices and programs must be kept up to date. Security patches are crucial to preventing corporate systems from becoming vulnerable to attacks. Financial firms should upgrade their ageing digital infrastructure and apply mobile device security. Any critical system or program that is not patched is a meaningful security risk for the entire corporation.

Principle 3. Create complex passwords and change them frequently

Creating complex passwords and changing them frequently is an important aspect of cyber-hygiene. Passwords should be strong and kept in secure locations. The use of different passwords for different applications as well as their frequent change increases cybersecurity. In that respect, the human factor should be taken into consideration. Most individuals typically choose passwords with a certain logic, which can be detected and calculated by specific machines. To counter that problem, consumer awareness regarding cyber-risk and the use of complex passwords are essential.[31]

Principle 4. Use micro-segmentation, multifactor authentication and encryption

Micro-segmentation, multifactor authentication and encryption of sensitive data are important and effective ingredients of cyber-hygiene. Micro-segmentation means that the corporate IT environment should be divided into several parts to make the entire system less vulnerable to cyberattacks. Multifactor authentication and encryption ensure that access to data is only granted to verified and eligible staff.

Principle 5. Implement the least privilege principle

Access to critical business and financial data should be based on the least privilege principle, which means that access to information is

---

[31] For instance, the use of passphrases consisting of unrelated words instead of passwords (e.g. book_zeppelin_perfume) could reinforce cybersecurity.

only provided on a 'need to know' basis. By keeping the number of employees and third-party contractors with data access at the necessary minimum, the risk of data breaches as well as the impact of a potential cyberattack can be reduced. The same principle should be applied to systems and programs, which should perform their tasks but nothing more.

Principle 6. Shadow IT: deal with rotting data and connections to third-party financial intermediaries

A large share of data possessed by financial firms is rotting and dark data, which is either partly or fully beyond the control of the corporate IT department. Therefore, the firms must secure their rotting and dark data. Furthermore, vulnerabilities can arise from connections to third-party financial intermediaries. Cyber-hygiene demands that organisations remain secure when they outsource activities. A layered approach with different measures on different levels is thus necessary to contain cyber-threats.

Principle 7. Establish an incident response and reporting plan

Financial organisations need to be prepared in case of cyber-incidents. This includes the design of appropriate cyber-response plans and mechanisms to combat cyberattacks. In addition, schemes need to be in place to decide about reporting and data sharing of cyber-incidents.

5.2   Use of certifications: A must-do?

The European economy increasingly depends on the frictionless use of ICT products and services. In recent years, these digital technologies have become more complex and more diverse, while at the same time the threat level of the cybersphere has increased. Firms and consumers using ICT products often do not have the knowledge to fully understand the cybersecurity dimension of the new technologies they use. Therefore, information asymmetries persist between software providers and software users, which could be detrimental to the effective functioning of the single market.

In order to limit the negative effects of this information asymmetry, some EU member states have put in place national cybersecurity certification schemes. These schemes attest that certified ICT products and services fulfil the most important cybersecurity standards. Table 4 presents national certification schemes that operate in the European Union.

One of the main issues with current national cybersecurity certification schemes is their high fragmentation and lack of mutual recognition by other member states, except for countries participating in the SOG-IS MRA framework. In addition, almost half of EU member states do not have a national cybersecurity certification scheme in place.

Table 4. Existing cybersecurity certification schemes in the EU

Existing certification schemes in the EU	Participating countries	Affected products, services or industries	Mutual recognition by other EU member states?
Commercial Product Assurance	United Kingdom	Commercial off-the-shelf products	No
Certification Sécuritaire de Premier Niveau	France	IT products and services	No
Baseline Security Product Assessment	The Netherlands	IT products and services	Unknown
SOG-IS MRA	Austria, Belgium, Croatia, Finland, France, Germany, Italy, Luxembourg, Norway, Poland, Spain, United Kingdom, Sweden	Digital products	Yes, but only for members of the scheme

Note: In addition to the four schemes described above, there are other emerging schemes in Germany, Italy and Sweden.
Source: Authors' compilation based on European Commission (2017), "Cybersecurity – EU Agency and Certification Framework", Factsheet (https://ec.europa.eu/digital-single-market/en/news/cybersecurity-eu-cybersecurity-agency-and-eu-framework-cybersecurity-certification).

Against this background, the European Commission announced in September 2017 its regulatory proposal for a European Cybersecurity Certification Scheme, as one of the core initiatives of the Cybersecurity Package. The Certification Scheme is expected to define common standards, procedures and technical requirements. While remaining voluntary, it would benefit from recognition by all member states, thereby addressing the issue of fragmentation.

The Commission's plan for the new scheme is to be operated by a new EU Cybersecurity Agency, for which ENISA shall be revised and equipped with a permanent mandate as well as more financial and human resources. Aside from harmonisation, the core objective is to strengthen Europe's cyber-resilience capabilities.[32]

Yet there remain important challenges regarding the Commission's proposal, as it raises many questions about the pros and cons of a European Cybersecurity Certification Scheme. Can the new European Certification Framework achieve the desired harmonisation or would it rather add another layer of complexity to the existing system? Can voluntary certification effectively increase Europe's cyber-resilience capabilities? Does ENISA have the required resources to fulfil the role of a certification agency? And, most important, is the private sector in general, and financial institutions in particular, likely to accept and participate in the new voluntary scheme?

Firstly, the regulatory proposal has the European Cybersecurity Certification Scheme superseding existing national frameworks and thereby setting common standards while reducing fragmentation and information asymmetries. In principle, such a "one-stop shop" system with mutual recognition by member states sounds desirable. However, there is a risk that the new European framework could add another layer of complexity and thereby further increase fragmentation.

---

[32] Proposal for a Regulation of the European Parliament and of the Council on ENISA, the "EU Cybersecurity Agency", and repealing Regulation (EU) 526/2013, and on Information and Communication Technology cybersecurity certification ("Cybersecurity Act") (https://ec.europa.eu/info/law/better-regulation/initiatives/com-2017-477_en).

For instance, it remains unclear what the role and responsibilities of a revised ENISA as the certifying agency will be in the existing structure of supervisory authorities such as the ECB and EBA.[33] The regulatory proposal foresees the member states being responsible for "supervisory, monitoring and enforcement tasks". Instead of centralisation and harmonisation, this will likely increase complexity.[34]

Secondly, a European certification could indeed raise the awareness of firms and citizens in respect of cybersecurity-related issues. Yet there is a risk of a false sense of security if software users regard their products as secure simply because they are certified. As emphasised earlier in this report, cybersecurity can be enhanced if firms and consumers embrace prevention, especially by following the principles of cyber-hygiene. If they care less about cybersecurity because their ICT products are certified, certification might trigger counterproductive effects.

Thirdly, the proposal should provide practical answers to the question of how the certification process intends to deal with the high diversity of products, services and processes in cybersecurity. The creation, constant updates and, potentially, supervision of the certification scheme is a complex and burdensome task, especially if ENISA would also be responsible for coordination and cooperation between the EU and member states. This requires adequate human and financial resources.

The Commission's plan to increase the budget from €11 million to €23 million and the number of staff from 84 to 125 over five years does not seem to be well-aligned with the large amount of products and services to be certified and the wide range of new tasks for the agency.[35] Operational concerns also persist regarding the agency's

---

[33] AFME (2018), "AFME Position Paper on the European Commission Cybersecurity Legislative Package" (https://ec.europa.eu/info/law/better-regulation/feedback/9045/attachment/090166e5b801caff_en).

[34] Page 11 of the Regulatory Proposal.

[35] European Commission (2017), "Cybersecurity – EU Agency and Certification Framework", Factsheet (https://ec.europa.eu/digital-single-market/en/news/cybersecurity-eu-cybersecurity-agency-and-eu-framework-cybersecurity-certification).

necessary sensitivity and trust, as business secrets might need to be disclosed during the certification process.[36] While clearly unintended, the collection of information on ICT products, services and business practices could render ENISA a valuable target for cyberattacks.

Fourthly, the certification process needs to keep up with the fast pace of technological change in the digital sphere. Cybersecurity-related issues are volatile and change rapidly over time. The Commission's proposal foresees certificates being valid for five years, but the practical question of how these certificates can reflect and integrate changes over time remains unanswered. Do (time-critical) software updates and patches need to be recertified? If so, the certification process might eventually appear rather unpractical and cost-inefficient. Furthermore, recertification would likely lead to a time delay until software users are able to update their systems, which could be harmful to cybersecurity.

Fifthly, *a priori* the most important condition for the success of a European Cybersecurity Certification Scheme is large-scale private sector engagement, as the new scheme would be voluntary. Widespread private sector acceptance can only be achieved if the value added of the new certification framework exceeds the costs of certification.[37] These costs can be significant, as shown by other certification schemes. Higher prices for ICT products and services could be the consequence for consumers.

In conclusion, it remains unclear whether a European Cybersecurity Certification Scheme is desirable. The current proposal reflects high ambitions but falls short of providing a holistic concept as to how these objectives can be achieved. For the certification framework to be successful, its value added must be greater than the additional costs. In its current form, the proposed framework's weaknesses seem to outweigh its potential advantages.

---

[36] AFME (2018), "AFME Position Paper on the European Commission Cybersecurity Legislative Package", (https://ec.europa.eu/info/law/better-regulation/feedback/9045/attachment/090166e5b801caff_en).

[37] Digital Europe (2017), "DIGITALEUROPE's views on Cybersecurity Certification and Labelling Schemes", www.digitaleurope.org/DesktopModules/Bring2mind/DMX/Download.aspx?Command=Core_Download&entryID=2365&language=en-US&PortalId=0&TabId=353.

6. COMPLEMENTARY POLICIES TO STRENGTHEN RESPONSES IN CASE OF CYBERATTACKS

6.1 Attribution and criminalisation: Reinforcing cross-border cooperation and legal convergence

When cyberattacks occur, two of their characteristics make their management particularly delicate: their global dimension and increasing sophistication.

The Internet has been developed on the back of a 'no boundaries principle'. All its autonomous systems speak a common language, which is a set of data formatting, naming, addressing and routing standards collectively known as "the internet protocols" (Mueller, 2017).[38] The most basic of these is Internet Protocol (IP). As such, cyberspace has been growing by ensuring technical compatibility on a global scale.

Because cyberspace is primarily global, cybercrime respects no border. It is likely that a significant share of cyberattacks is shaped and launched on a cross-border basis. A cybercriminal in country A can have colleagues in country B, use servers in country C and targets users in country D.

Given the complexity of these attacks, it is highly difficult to compile robust statistics on the provenance and destination of cyberattacks. Some researchers have been trying to develop relevant

---

[38] See www.wiley.com/en-be/Will+the+Internet+Fragment%3F:+Sovereignty,+Globalization+and+Cyberspace-p-9781509501229

proxies, such as the use of a global network of honeypots,[39] to detect and assess the volume of active reconnaissance[40] by hackers (F-secure, 2017).[41]

Some statistics developed by F-secure revealed that cross-border active reconnaissance within the EU originated well outside of EU borders. In the second half of 2016, it was believed that the main source countries in terms of IP addresses were, in order of importance: Russia, the Netherlands, the US, Germany and China. Most countries were targeted by Russian IPs, including Russia. The US, the Netherlands, Germany, China and the UK were the top target countries for attacks on the honeypot network.

The will of financial firms to handle cross-border attacks has been tested by severe challenges. First, in the wake of an attack, attribution often results from a complex, costly and lengthy process, frequently involving external experts and local authorities.[42] The task proves to be even more complex on a cross-border basis, as exchanges of information between countries concerning cybersecurity matters have been thus far poorly regulated and generally require the use of "official" bureaucratic channels.

Should the attribution be successful, the criminalisation of perpetrators proves to be another daunting task. Given the lack of harmonisation in cybercrime laws, perpetrators are often inclined to seek refuge in countries where there are no, or insufficient, cybercrime laws to implement an extradition request. Also, as analysed by Hakmeh (2017),[43] many countries have double criminality requirement, implying that a suspect can be extradited

---

[39] Honeypot is a computer security mechanism set to detect, deflect or, in some manner, counteract attempts at unauthorised use of information systems.

[40] Active reconnaissance is a type of computer attack in which an intruder engages with the targeted system to gather information about vulnerabilities.

[41] The publication can be found at hwww.f-secure.com/documents/996508/1030743/cybersecurity-report-2017

[42] Attribution is the process of tracking down and identifying those responsible for a cyberattack. It is becoming more important for investigators and intelligence analysts to track down those responsible, whether a person, group or country.

[43] See www.chathamhouse.org/expert/comment/building-stronger-international-legal-framework-cybercrime?gclid=EAIaIQobChMIyraq0bW-2QIVjp3tCh0LBwLcEAAYASAAEgJdlfD_BwE.

to stand trial in a foreign country for breaking its law only if there is a similar law criminalising that offence in the extraditing country. As such, should relevant laws not be in harmony between investigating states, perpetrators can roam free.

Against this background, there is an urgent need for policy-makers and supervisors to develop a framework that greatly facilitates the exchange of information and electronic evidence for the purpose of cybercrime prevention, investigation and prosecution. When the criminals behind cross-border attacks are identified, there is a need for convergence in national legal frameworks in order to facilitate their extradition.

In April 2018, the European Commission proposed new rules whose objective is to make it easier and less time-consuming for police and judicial authorities to access the electronic evidence they need in investigations to catch and convict criminals and terrorists.[44] Such proposed legislation should contribute to facilitate the investigation and criminalisation related to cyberattacks in the financial sector. An ambitious approach for the case of cross-border requests of electronic evidence would be essential for this legislation to contribute fully to better treatment of cross-border cyberattacks.

6.2 Best practices in remedies in case of cyberattacks

The damage inflicted by large cyberattacks can be significant for both financial firms and clients. While major insurers nowadays offer cybersecurity insurance to firms, consumers are usually uninsured against cybersecurity risks. As demonstrated by the case study in Box 1, cyberattacks such as the hacking of Tesco Bank's online banking system impact consumers through financial fraud and/or identity theft. This poses an important question of remedies for cyberattacks. What are the legal and regulatory consequences of cyberattacks in which, for example, consumer current accounts have been misappropriated and/or personal data have been stolen?

---

[44] The proposal can be found at https://ec.europa.eu/info/policies/justice-and-fundamental-rights/criminal-justice/e-evidence-cross-border-access-electronic-evidence_en.

The first challenge is to clarify the degree to which clients and/or providers share the liability for the hack. Secondly, a distinction can be made between financial fraud on clients' accounts and the theft of data. The former results in immediate financial losses for the affected consumers or firms. The latter impacts the clients' rights as the data could later on be used for identity theft and eventually incur financial losses to clients. Thirdly, the best remedies for each situation need to be assessed.

While both financial institutions and consumers are victims of cyberattacks, questions remain as to how to assess whether mistakes or negligence on the side of one party or both parties is partly responsible for the occurrence of an attack. As emphasised by De Werra et al. (2018),[45] the civil liability resulting from such attacks raises complex legal issues because of the diversity of potentially applicable liability regimes (personal data protection, product liability regulations, etc.). Regulatory standards of "reasonable cybersecurity measures" can vary, depending on the context and the nature of the affected data. In addition, assessing the liability can be challenging when a chain of parties may have contributed to the attack and its spread, whether or not they did it unintentionally.

Specifically to the financial sector, Articles 73 and 74 of PSD2 provide some elements in the context of an unauthorised transaction. If it is proved that consumers can be blamed for the unauthorised transaction, financial firms are nevertheless required to bear their consumers' financial losses after notification. However, consumers can be held accountable by their banks for a share of the financial damage, up to €50.

If the liability for the unauthorised transaction lies with providers, however, PSPs are required to immediately refund the financial losses on their customers' accounts. For both cases, the regulatory standards set by PSD2 are generally favourable to consumers, as their PSPs have to bear the financial damage in any case, with the exception of the €50 threshold in case of consumer liability (see Article 74 of PSD2).

---

[45] See De Werra J. and E. Studer (2017), "Regulating cybersecurity: What civil liability in case of cyber-attacks?" (https://papers.ssrn.com/sol3/papers.cfm?abstract_id=3022522).

Taking a closer look at the case of liability on the side of PSPs, according to PSD2, PSPs are only required to follow the minimal principle of "what is lost is due". As regards additional compensation, Article 73 (3) of PSD2 emphasises:

> Further financial compensation may be determined in accordance with the law applicable to the contract concluded between the payer and the payment service provider or the contract concluded between the payer and the payment initiation service provider if applicable.

Therefore, the right of consumers for additional compensation remains vague in PSD2. Questions arise as to how and to which extent customers can be compensated for the inconvenience resulting from an unauthorised transaction, such as the inability to use a payment card for a certain time or the temporary shutdown of all operations and services. Those non-financial consequences can be severe, as the Tesco Bank case study demonstrates. Further investigation of the pros and cons of the creation of a more systematic compensation mechanism would be desirable.

The question of liability and appropriate remedies also concerns cyberattacks that target data theft. Stealing personal data usually does not directly inflict financial damage, but it does impact consumer rights, as the data could for instance later be used for identity theft, which in turn could possibly be leveraged for financial fraud. Under the current regulatory environment of PSD2 and GDPR, financial firms that suffer data theft are required to report these data breaches to their supervisors and consumers within a given time frame.

Yet in order to encourage best practices, financial firms should not only notify their customers but follow up on the actual damage. In that respect, Article 82 (1) of GDPR emphasises that:

> Any person who has suffered material or non-material damage as a result of an infringement of this Regulation shall have the right to receive compensation from the controller or processor for the damage suffered.

Different examples of damages are notably provided in the Recital (75) of the regulation and can concern damage to the reputation, loss of confidentiality of personal data, etc. The scope of the liability is clearly defined in the Article 82 of the GDPR, as it concerns only cases where the Regulation has been infringed. However, it remains challenging to properly quantify the damage resulting from a data theft. In that respect, as is the case for additional compensation in the context of unauthorised transactions, should a more systematic compensation mechanism be developed?

In its communication on "Building A European Data Economy" (2017),[46] the European Commission emphasised its objective "to enhance legal certainty with regard to liability in the context of emerging technologies and thereby create favourable conditions for innovation". The development of a legislative framework where "liability could be" systematically "assigned to the market players generating a major risk for others or to those market players which are best placed to minimise or avoid the realisation of such risk",[47] might motivate firms to reinforce the quality of their cyber-infrastructures. It could also impede innovation, however, as the more innovative the financial firm might be in employing digital technologies, the more exposed it could become to lawsuits.

Since financial firms need to comply with PSD2 and GDPR, the coming years will provide a good opportunity to assess best practices in terms of liability allocation and remedies in the financial sector. Court cases and regular monitoring of these elements could help EU and national supervisors to compile a list of best principles that could be regularly adjusted in response to the rapidly changing cyber-landscape.

---

[46] See on page 15 of the Communication of the European Commission on "Building A European Data Economy", 2017 (https://eur-lex.europa.eu/legal-content/EN/TXT/PDF/?uri=CELEX:52017DC0009&from=EN).

[47] In its Communication, the European Commission called these approaches the "risk-generating or risk-management approaches". The European Commission also mentioned the voluntary or mandatory insurance schemes. Such schemes could be coupled with the above-mentioned liability approaches. They would compensate the parties who suffered the damage (e.g. the consumer). This approach would need to provide legal protection to investments made by business while reassuring victims regarding fair compensation or appropriate insurance in case of damage.

In particular, these principles should cover the use of robust methodologies to assess the degree to which firms and/or clients share the cyber-liability. They should also help firms assess when consumer financial compensation that goes beyond the actual financial loss incurred should be provided. Finally, these principles should also provide guidelines on the best type of remedies in case of data theft without immediate financial loss.

6.3   Is an emergency fund needed in case of large cyberattacks?

In its impact assessment conducted in connection with the Cybersecurity Package, the Commission mentioned the possibility of developing an EU Cybersecurity Emergency Fund.[48] This fund was defined as follows:

> The EU Cybersecurity Emergency Fund is an initiative developed in the context of the review of the Cybersecurity Strategy on the example of existing crisis mechanisms in other EU policy areas. It will provide the possibility for Member States to seek help at the EU level in case of major incident. It could be used to support, directly or indirectly, citizens, companies or public administrations hit by cyberattacks.

In an interview he gave on the occasion of presenting the Cybersecurity Package (13 September 2017),[49] Commissioner Andrus Ansip made a parallel with the "need for emergency funding in case of a hurricane or an earthquake". According to him, "It is the same story with large-scale cyber-attacks". As regards the financial sector, the main advantage of an emergency cyber-fund would be to alleviate financial stability risk in case of major cyberattacks. The development of a fund to help financial firms recover from cyberattacks raises specific questions and needs to address specific issues.

---

[48] See Impact Assessment SWD(2017)500/948161- Part 1 (https://ec.europa.eu/info/law/better-regulation/initiatives/com-2017-477_en).

[49] See Euractiv's analysis of this speech (www.euractiv.com/section/cybersecurity/news/ansip-member-states-will-need-help-from-eu-cyber-emergency-fund/).

What type of damages could be funded?

The impact assessment of the European Commission mentioned a few types of actions that could be funded through this fund:

> The Fund could deploy a rapid response capability in the interests of solidarity and finance specific emergency response actions such as replacing compromised equipment or deploying mitigation or response tools to assist victims.

Echoing the findings of section 3.1, a proper estimation of the financial impacts of large cyberattacks will be needed. These statistics should contribute to shaping the fund and estimating the required aggregate amounts.

Should existing EU schemes for natural disasters be extended to large-scale cyberattacks?

EU support in case of natural disasters has been recently strengthened through the launch of a new EU financial mechanism in July 2017.[50] Member states affected by a natural disaster can activate this special EU financial mechanism and fund reconstruction operations with an exceptional EU co-financing rate of 95% under a cohesion policy programme, instead of the programme's normal co-financing. The EU needs to assess the possibility of extending existing EU funding schemes for natural disasters to large-scale cyberattacks.

Cyber-incident criteria

One of the main questions concerns the type of incident for which a special fund could be used. The term "major incidents" emphasised in the impact assessment could use the definition provided in the Blueprint of the European Commission on Coordinated Response to Large Scale Cybersecurity Incidents and Crises (2017):[51]

> A cybersecurity incident affecting organisations in more than one Member State or even the entire Union with

---

[50] Details on the EU initiative can be found at http://ec.europa.eu/ regional_policy/en/newsroom/news/2017/07/27-07-2017-special-eu-support-in-case-of-natural-disasters-enters-into-force-today

[51] The Blueprint can be found at http://ec.europa.eu/transparency/regdoc/ rep/3/2017/EN/C-2017-6100-F1-EN-MAIN-PART-1.PDF

potential serious disruptions to the internal market and more broadly to the network and information systems on which the Union economy, democracy and society rely on... A cybersecurity incident may be considered a crisis at Union level when the disruption caused by the incident is too extensive for a concerned Member State to handle on its own or when it affects two or more Member States with such a wide-ranging impact of technical or political significance that it requires timely coordination and response at Union political level.

Another criterion could concern the role of private insurance. Once all private insurance options have been exhausted, then the EU scheme could be activated. This would notably concern very large attacks that insurance companies are unable to handle.

Whatever criteria are chosen for a successful cyberattack to qualify, the authority in charge of the fund will need to be able to assess very rapidly whether these criteria are fulfilled following a request to use the fund. Speed is indeed essential to ensuring an efficient response to a large scale attack.

Box 2. Can cyberattacks be systemic?

In recent years, one of the most intense debates with respect to cybersecurity has been over whether a systemic cyberattack can occur or is more myth than reality. Systemic risk is generally defined as the possibility that an event at the company level could trigger severe instability or collapse an entire industry or economy.

The understanding of the systemic risk has been significantly refined since the financial crisis of 2008. Two types of financial firms can be considered a systemic risk. The first concerns very large financial corporations and is often called "too big to fail". The second relates to organisations that are highly interconnected with others. Systemic risk occurs when one firm considered "too big to fail" and/or "too connected to fail" collapses or is on the verge of doing so. Given the connectivity of such financial firms with the rest of the financial sector and the economy, the crisis can rapidly spread to most of the sector, thereby raising markedly financial instability and risks of other collapses.

Typically, large financial crises are triggered by the economic behaviours of agents. For example, resulting from inadequate investments and/or sharp macroeconomic reversals, the publication of much higher than expected financial losses for a systemic bank could trigger a panic among a large share of investors and savers. The loss of confidence of agents in the ability of the bank to recover could result in bank runs (a large share of savers withdraw their liquidity) and the freezing of credit on the interbank market, as other banks believe the affected bank cannot reimburse them. Given the high interconnectedness between financial firms, the eventual collapse of the affected firm could result in a rapid propagation of the crisis to many other firms.

The question is therefore whether a large cyberattack can affect one or several financial firms to an extent that economic agents lose confidence in the former's ability to recover in the medium and long term. Major cyberattacks have already paralysed the IT systems of large financial firms via large-scale DoS, but generally during a limited period of time or within a specific part of the firm.

So far, no cyberattack in the financial sector has approached what can be called a systemic risk. At worst, massive theft of consumer data, as was the case with Equifax, can raise serious concerns about the long term viability of the Internet. Yet this type of large attack has not resulted in significant economic disturbances.

Does it mean that cyberattacks and systemic risk are and will remain two distinct elements in the financial sector? In our ever-changing world, this bet would be too risky to take. A very wide DoS paralysing most of the IT infrastructure of a few systemic banks could eventually result in a large loss of confidence among economic agents, thereby leading to serious economic disturbances. Should such a cyberattack occur during a large financial crisis, when economic agents have already lost significant confidence, then perhaps the systemic impact could become reality.

What conditions must be respected?

One of the main disadvantages of an EU Cybersecurity Emergency Fund concerns the problem of moral hazard. As their costs in case of attacks could be covered by the fund, some financial firms might be less cautious regarding the quality of their cybersecurity defences. There is therefore a risk that the establishment of a fund for cyber-incidents would alter the willingness of some financial firms to reinforce their cyber-resilience.

Against this background, the most appropriate approach to solving the problem of moral hazard is defining several clear conditions for using the fund. Some possible remedies to address the problem of moral hazard have already been added to the impact assessment of the European Commission (2017). According to the assessment, member states could have access to such a fund only if:

> They had put in place a prudent system of cybersecurity prior to the incident, including full implementation of the NIS Directive, mature risk management and respective supervisory frameworks at national level.

Could a fund designed specifically for the financial sector be the solution?

A parallel could be drawn with the Single Resolution Fund established in 2014. This fund can be used by the Single Resolution Board in order to ensure the efficient application of resolution tools and the exercise of the resolution powers conferred to the Single Resolution Board for the management of large banks in financial distress. The fund can be used only when the bank needs to be resolved. One particularity of the resolution fund is that it is fully funded by financial firms.[52] Should a similar fund be established for cyber-risks in the financial sector only?

In the financial sector, cyberattacks should be approached in accordance with their potential impact on financial stability. So far, as shown in Box 1, no successful cyberattack has managed to trigger systemic risks in the financial sector. Yet, no one knows if this will happen in the future. Overall, given the still ambiguous relationship between cyber-risks and systemic risk in the financial sector, there is no sufficient ground to develop an emergency cyber-fund only for the financial sector. It should be up to banks to decide whether to do so.

What about a fund for all operators of essential services?

Should an emergency cyber-fund be designed for specific sectors or stakeholders, one possibility would be to extend it to all operators that have already been assessed as critical for cybersecurity. The NIS

---

[52] Information on the Resolution Fund can be found at https://srb.europa.eu/en/content/single-resolution-fund

(2016), for example, asked member states to list operators of essential services in seven sectors: energy (electricity), transport (air, rail, water and road), banking (credit institutions), financial market infrastructure (trading venues, central counterparties), health (healthcare settings), water (drinking water supply and distribution) and digital infrastructure (Internet exchange points, domain name system service providers, top-level domain name registries). One option for the EU would be to assess the possibility and need of developing a hybrid fund combining private and public funding for these different operators.

CONCLUSIONS

As cyberattacks increase in sophistication, the EU cyber package provides the right opportunity to develop an ambitious EU cyber-policy in the financial sector. However, several issues still need to be addressed to raise the cyber-resilience of financial firms and improve the response in case of attacks.

The emergence of a coherent cyber-policy for financial firms will require the clear definition of the roles and responsibilities of the parties involved: end-users, industry, regulators and supervisors. In order to reduce cybercrime, consumers should practise cyber-hygiene whenever relevant and possible. Cyber-education and consumer awareness are key to promoting this behaviour.

Good governance is essential within financial firms. Well-informed boards that understand cyber-threats can set a realistic risk appetite and challenge their executives with good quality management information. This notably implies the promotion of cyber-hygiene at all levels of the organisation, as well as the continuous sharing of relevant information with authorities and other firms.

Regulators should ensure that the most adequate rules and institutional frameworks are in place to boost the cyber-resilience of financial firms. Regulators need to be agile to respond to the ever-changing nature of cyberspace. While the prevention of cyberattacks and the reinforcement of cyber-resilience are the key objectives of regulators and supervisors, rules still need to be created and reinforced to shape mechanisms in case of attacks. In particular, this report emphasises the need to improve the processes for attribution, extradition, emergency funding and remedies.

Supervisors should support the information sharing on cybersecurity issues and ensure incident reporting requirements can significantly contribute to the cyber-resilience of financial firms. This could imply that specific cyber-bodies would play the role of technical advisers. In order to be fully operational, one cyber-agency would need a clear mandate from regulators on the nature of their missions and on the types of tools they can use to achieve their objectives.

ANNEX -
TASK FORCE MEMBERS,
OBSERVERS AND SPEAKERS

Chairman:	**Richard Parlour** Principal, Financial Markets Law International
Rapporteur:	**Sylvain Bouyon** Research Fellow, Head of Fintech and Retail Finance, CEPS and ECRI
	Simon Krause Visiting Researcher, CEPS

Task Force Members

Jean Allix, Special Adviser, BEUC

Simona Autolitano, Policy Coordinator, Microsoft

Sue Basu, Senior Policy Advisor, Visa Europe

Bob Bekker, Information Security Professional, ING

Elie Beyrouthy, Vice President, European Government Affairs, American Express

Christophe Bonte, Senior Advisor, Swiss Finance Council

Axel Bysikiewicz, Attorney at Law, Schufa Holding AG

Anne Chauviré, Officer, BNP Paribas Personal Finance

Christine Colaert, Responsable lobbying juridique et veille légale et réglementaire, Cofidis

Willem-Pieter De Groen, Research Fellow and Head of Unit, CEPS

Jean-Eric De Mesmay, Director (International Development), Cofidis

Raffaella Donnini, Head of European Growth Policy office, Intesa Sanpaolo

Paloma Garcia, Consultant, Afore Consulting

Liam Gibbon, President, Moody's

Isabelle Guittard-Losay, Head of Institutional Relationship, BNP Paribas Personal Finance

Anne-Gabrielle Haie, Lawyer, DLA Piper UK LLP

Brit Hecht, Senior Policy Advisor, Banco Bilbao Vizcaya Argentaria (BBVA)

Marc Hemmerling, General Counsel Digital Transformation, Fintech and Payments, ABBL

Stevi Iosif, Associate Director, AFME

Karel Lannoo, CEO, CEPS

Otso Manninen, Economist, Bank of Finland

Monica Monaco, Founder and Managing Director TrustEU Affairs

Jan Neutze, Director of Cybersecurity Policy, Microsoft

Valerijus Ostrovskis, Lead Lawyer, DLA Piper

Maximilian Siemens, EU Public Policy Programme Officer, TrustEuAffairs

Mark Smitham, Senior Manager of Cybersecurity Policy, Microsoft

Michalis Sotiropoulos, Director, The Depository & Clearing Corporation (DTCC)

Paul Thomalla, SVP Global Corporate Relations, ACI Worldwide

Kim Vindberg-Larsen, CEO, MEEuniversal ApS

Urte Von Raczeck, Manager International Business, Schufa Holding AG

Task Force Observers

Oliver Cusworth, Policy Advisor, European Investment Bank

Angelos Delivorias, Policy Analyst, European Parliament

Jean-Luc Filippini, Senior Policy Advisor, European Investment Bank

Nicholas Herbert-Young, Communications & International Division, Financial Conduct Authority

Robin Jones, Head of Technology, Resilience & Cyber Specialist Supervision, Financial Conduct Authority

Lazaros Panourgias, Head EIF Affairs, Brussels, European Investment Fund

Cyril Schlund, Economist, European Central Bank

Invited Speakers

Kick-off meeting: 19 September 2017 – Definition of the scope

Lorenzo Pupillo, Associate Senior Research Fellow and Head of the Cybersecurity@CEPS Initiative

Bruno Schröder, National Technology Officer, Microsoft Belux

Erik Van Zuuren, Founder, TrustCore.eu

Simon Wilkinson, Operating Director, Tradle

Second meeting: 20 November 2017

Pierre Chastanet, Deputy Head of Cloud and Software, European Commission, DG CONNECT

Sébastien De Brouwer, Chief Policy Officer, European Banking Federation

Maniati Alexandra, Senior Policy Adviser, Social Affairs and Cybersecurity, European Banking Authority

Third meeting: 6 February 2018

Jakub Boratyński, Head of Trust and Security, European Commission, DG Connect

Rasmus Theede, Managing Partner, DigitalNations

David Porter, Associate Partner, IBM

Grégoire Issenmann, Head of Section, SSM Risk Analysis Division, ECB

Fourth meeting: 17 May 2018 - finalisation of the report

www.ingramcontent.com/pod-product-compliance
Lightning Source LLC
Chambersburg PA
CBHW020359270326
41926CB00007B/502